# Prescot of Yesteryear

BY ARTHUR S ROBERTS

SHEARWATER

Sponsored by Shearwater, developers of
the Prescot Centre, which opened in 1989.

*By the same author*

Prescot When I was a Boy
(published1987)

*Prescot of Yesteryear copyright © 1990 by Arthur S Roberts.*
*ISBN 0 9515986 0 0*
*First printed 1990. All rights reserved. No part of this publication may be reproduced or transmitted in any form or by any means without prior permission in writing from Arthur S Roberts, 19 Queens Road, Prescot, Merseyside L34 6JA. Tel: (051) 426 5614.* *Prescot of Yesteryear was designed and produced By Steve Goddard Media Services and Clark & Clark Design Studios, Commercial Business Centre, Kendrick's Cross, Rainhill, Merseyside L35 4LP and distributed by Countyvise Ltd, 1 and 3 Grove Road, Rock Ferry, Birkenhead, Wirral, Merseyside L42 3XS. TEL (051) 645 2311.*

*Printed by: Allied Publicity*

*Cover illustration by Steve Kelly,from a print of Eccleston Street, Prescot. Circa 1905.*

# PRESCOT OF YESTERYEAR

## Contents


| | |
|---|---|
| Foreword | 5 |
| Acknowledgements | 7 |
| Introduction | 8 |
| Origins of Prescot | 9 |
| Turnpike Roads | 11 |
| | |
| 1 The Church and its environs | 14 |
| 2 Market Place, Sewell Street and Hall Lane | 22 |
| 3 Kemble Street | 29 |
| 4 Eccleston Street | 35 |
| 5 Derby Street | 40 |
| 6 High Street | 46 |
| 7 Highfield Place | 52 |
| 8 Courts, wients, passages etc. | 57 |
| 9 St Helens Road | 66 |
| 10 Warrington Road | 71 |
| 11 Beaconsfield | 73 |
| 12 Aspinall Street | 82 |
| 13 Reminders of a bygone age | 84 |
| 14 Industries in Prescot | 91 |
| 15 Index | 93 |

# FOREWORD

As a recent resident of Prescot and the town's M.P., I am well aware of the fascinating history of Prescot. It is fortunate indeed that Arthur Roberts, a life long Prescotian, has taken on the task of recording both visually and in words, how Prescot has developed over the years.

Part of an appreciation of the present must rest on how we understand the past and this is always a justification for taking an interest in history. Arthur's book is in the finest tradition of local historians, in that it sets history into a context which is readily understandable to anyone who knows Prescot.

'Prescot of Yesteryear' has most certainly enriched my own appreciation of the town in which I live. I am sure it will have exactly the same effect for every other resident or, indeed, anyone who is a student of local history.

Rt. Hon. George Howarth M.P.

Prescot of Yesteryear
Eccleston Street, Prescot. Circa 1905.

Prescot of Today
Eccleston Street, Prescot 1990.

# ACKNOWLEDGEMENTS

There is ample evidence that a revival of interest in what is happening in Prescot today is gaining strength. It has been obvious to me that over a long period people have developed a keenness to know more about the history of our growth as an ancient township which was of significant importance within the North West. The pity seems to be that this interest, and the means of implementing it, were not forthcoming earlier. All, however, is not completely lost, and a resurgence in an appreciation of our heritage even at this late stage is better than none at all. In the preparation of this work, and that of previous efforts which I have undertaken, I have been vastly encouraged by the help afforded by very many people. My gratitude is due to my wife Alice for her patience and loyal support, and to my step-daughter, Miss Alison J. Bibby (B.A. Hons.) whose help has been considerable.

The Library Service of the Metropolitan Borough of Knowsley, and in particular Mr T.W. Scragg, M.A., B. Phil., his assistant Mr W. Lund, and Mr Bill Bygroves merit special mention. So do members of the Prescot Historic Society, their Archivist, Miss Mavis Abraham, and the countless people who have placed photographs at my disposal which I have been able to use.

There is always a danger of omitting the names of people who have assisted in any way. I hope that I shall not fall into that trap, and apologise for any such oversight. Those who have provided negatives and prints and other material include:-

National Galleries and Museums on Merseyside, Prescot Historic Society, the Local Studies Section of Huyton Library, Mr W.H. Quick, Mr H. Edwards, Mr W. Coombs, the late Mr Jack Knowles, Mr R. Metcalfe, Mr Bert Taylor, Mr. W. Pennington, The Prescot Reporter, Lancashire Life, the late G.G. Hemingway, Mr H. Glover, and the Walker Art Gallery.

Above all I am grateful to Mr D.L. Shaw, FRICS, Director of Shearwater, the developers of the Prescot Centre, for his interest and generous financial backing of this project and also to Steve Goddard and Dave Clark for their invaluable assistance.

I an indebted to them all.

A.S. Roberts,
19 Queens Road,
Prescot.

February 1990

# INTRODUCTION

The inexorable passage of time brings many changes to locations, structures and associations which many of us hold dear.

We cannot stand in the way of progress, nor, if we are sure that developments can be truly classed as progress, would we wish to do so.

In the space of a lifetime so many of the features of the place that natives of Prescot call home, have been eroded. Changes are currently taking place which will render recognition of old landmarks difficult, if not impossible.

Few people would claim that our town is a place of outstanding beauty, but to countless thousands of people, over a long period of time, it represents home and roots, which are dear to us all.

There is a growing awareness today that treasures of the past have been irrevocably lost, so such momentoes as can be assembled under one cover must have a value in preserving the town's identity.

In the light of recent redevelopment of the town of Prescot, culminating in the opening of the fine new shopping and civic centre, it is timely that a review of the place as it once was in former days should be set down.

If the compilation of such a document as this serves to recall what we consider to be our heritage, it will have served its purpose well.

A.S. Roberts

# ORIGINS OF PRESCOT

The ancient ecclesiastical parish of Prescot was one of the most extensive in south-west Lancashire. It comprised an area of 36,554 statute acres. When the boundaries of Lichfield diocese were redefined, Prescot became part of the diocese of Chester and the Archdeaconry of Liverpool (before the latter became a separate diocese) and was a Deanery in its own right.

The name derives from the Saxon 'Preost' - a priest, and 'Cote, Coit and Cot' a building of wood. An earlier name by which the place was known was Churchley. A ley or leigh denoted a clearing in the forest. This clearing was made by the inhabitants and on it a church was erected. In the course of time the name Churchley was abandoned, except in such connections as plots of land e.g. Churchley Fields which surrounded the newly erected building. The present church is the fourth on this site. Now Priestcote, or in the latinised form Prestacota, became Prescot, by which the place is known to the present day.

In Volume Two of Baines History of the County of Lancashire we find a clear account of the extent of the parish, and the boundaries on all points of the compass.

On the south lay the river Mersey, whilst on the west and north-west it abutted on the parishes of Huyton and Walton. To the north lay the parish of Ormskirk. Wigan was its neighbour in the north-north-east, and on the east it was bounded by the parishes of Winwick and Warrington.

The extreme length of the parish of Prescot was twelve miles from Ditton in the south to Rainford in the north. Its breadth, from the town of Prescot in the west to Great Sankey in the east, was eight miles. This gives some idea of the size and importance, in earlier times, of a parish which had the township of Prescot as its centre.

The ancient manor of Prescot was presided over by the lord who delegated the duties of oversight to the rector. Although close links existed between this man and the church, not all rectors were men in holy orders. The abode of the rector was Prescot Hall.

In the reign of Henry VI, in the 15th century, the rectory was transferred to the new college in Cambridge, which we know as King's College, and from 1448 onwards vicars were appointed. The first of these was Ralph Duckworth and since his day, twenty-nine men have held the post. The present occupant is the Rev. Robert Sturman.

A favourite schoolboy translation of the adopted King's College coat of arms and motto, as applied to the old badge of Prescot Grammar School, "FLOREAT PRESCOTIA", was 'Let Prescot flourish'.

Although we acknowledge that we are an integral part of the Metropolitan Borough of Knowsley, we natives of the old town treasure the hope that, as an entity, we may long continue to flourish.

Prescot has no registered arms. Its badge has come from the arms of King's College, Cambridge which owned much of the land in Prescot and still has links with the area. The College's arms come from its founder, King Henry VI.

# THE TURNPIKE ROAD

In the 18th century the turnpike roads were opened, connecting Liverpool with Ashton-in-Makerfield and Warrington.

They followed the route of the present road from Liverpool Exchange, through Old Swan, Knotty Ash, Page Moss, Twig Lane, Blue Bell and Brook Bridge to Hackley Moss (near the King's Arms, Prescot). Here they divided, one part proceeding via Copt Holt, beyond the Green Dragon (Whiston), to Kenwright's Cross, Rainhill Stoops, through Bold Heath and Sankey to Bank Quay, Warrington.

The road through Prescot continued by way of Eccleston Lane Ends, Eccleston Hill, Bird i'th Hand, Eccleston Arms, Croppers Hill to Kitt's Bridge and St. Helens. Thence it proceeded past Parr Hall, Judgefield Brow, Ashton Cross and on to Ashton-in-Makerfield. Toll gates were in operation along both stretches of road.

Other lesser turnpikes interspersed the area. A loop to the main Turnpike leaving Old Swan followed Petticoat Lane through Broad Green, Roby, Blacklow Brow and on to the Blue Bell to join the main road.

Lesser roads and turnpikes were in evidence at that time, and by use of these the main turnpikes were reached.

The main route followed is similar to that of the A57 of to-day.

The whole of this system was administered by a Turnpike Trust.

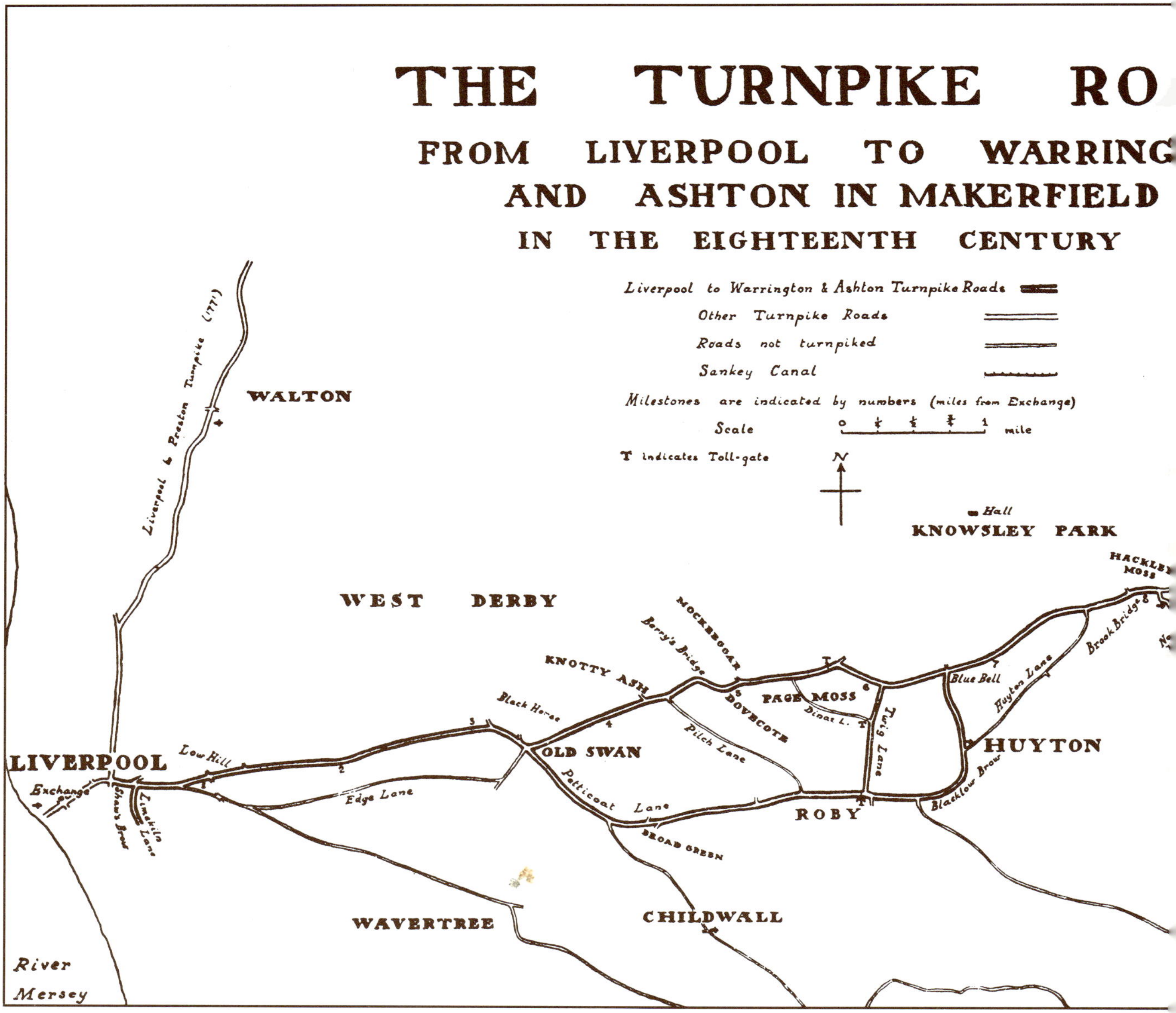
THE TURNPIKE RO
FROM LIVERPOOL TO WARRING
AND ASHTON IN MAKERFIELD
IN THE EIGHTEENTH CENTURY
Liverpool to Warrington & Ashton Turnpike Roads
Other Turnpike Roads
Roads not turnpiked
Sankey Canal
Milestones are indicated by numbers (miles from Exchange)
Scale
mile
T indicates Toll-gate
N
Hall
KNOWSLEY PARK
WALTON
Liverpool & Preston Turnpike (1771)
WEST DERBY
MOCKBEGGAR
Berry's Bridge
KNOTTY ASH
Black Horse
DOVECOTE
PAGE MOSS
Dinas L.
Pilch Lane
Twig Lane
Blue Bell
Huyton Lane
Brook Bridge
HUYTON
Blacklow Brow
LIVERPOOL
Low Hill
OLD SWAN
Exchange
Shaw's Brow
Limekiln Lane
Edge Lane
Petticoat Lane
ROBY
BROAD GREEN
WAVERTREE
CHILDWALL
River Mersey

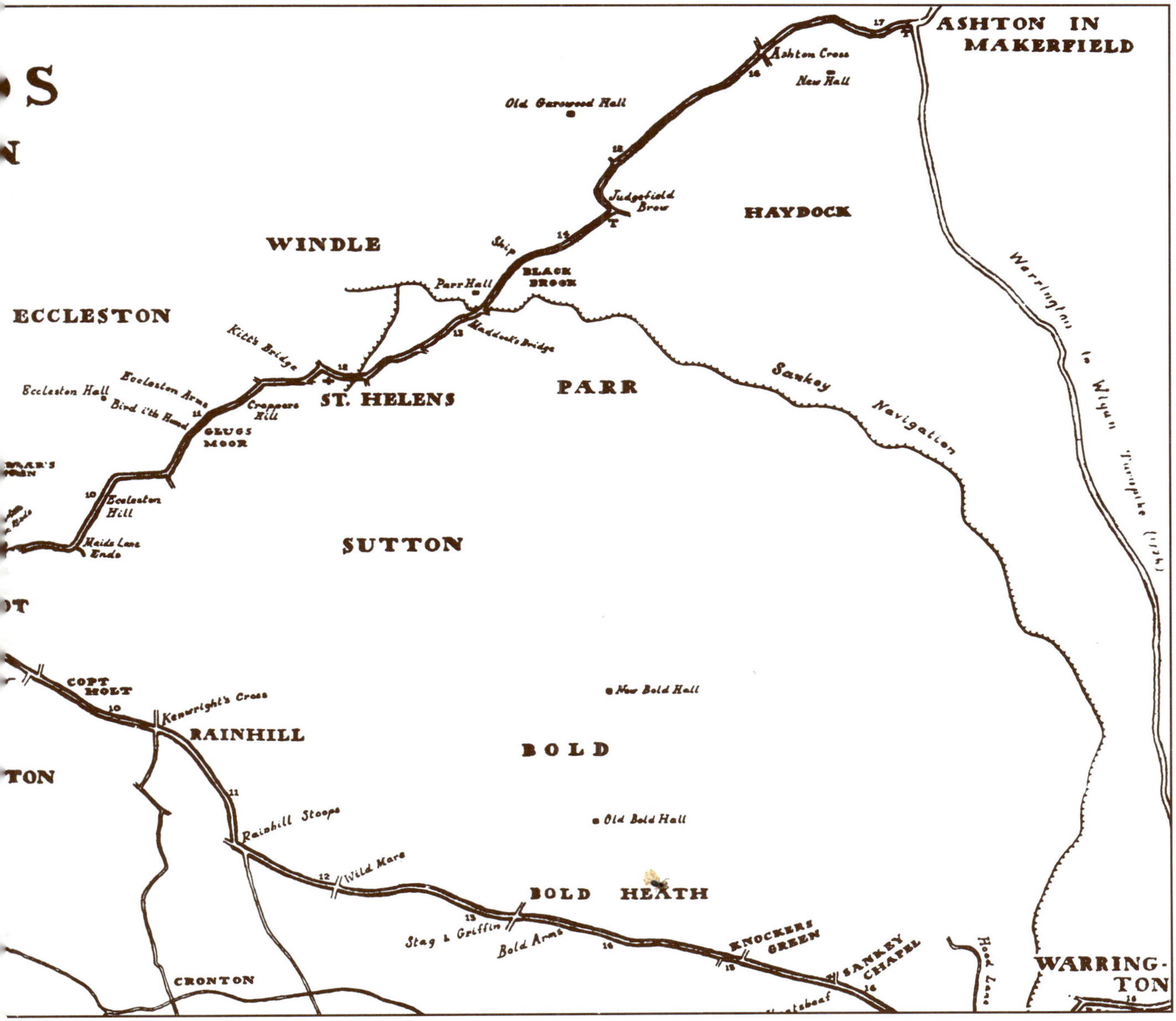
ASHTON IN MAKERFIELD
Ashton Cross
New Hall
Old Garswood Hall
Judgefield Brow
HAYDOCK
WINDLE
Ship
Parr Hall
BLACK BROOK
ECCLESTON
Kitt's Bridge
Eccleston Hall
Eccleston Arms
Bird i'th Hand
Croppers Hill
ST. HELENS
PARR
Sankey Navigation
Eccleston Hill
Maids Lane Ends
SUTTON
COPT HOLT
Kenwright's Cross
RAINHILL
New Bold Hall
BOLD
Rainhill Stoops
Old Bold Hall
Wild Mare
BOLD HEATH
Stag & Griffin
Bold Arms
KNOCKERS GREEN
SANKEY CHAPEL
Hood Lane
WARRINGTON
CRONTON

# CHAPTER ONE

## The Church and its environs

For centuries the Parish Church was the focal point of the town, and this to some extent is still the case. After the addition of the tower and spire in 1729, it became the subject of a number of photographs and sketches. These are used liberally here, and show the area during many periods of change, so far as the surroundings of the edifice are concerned.

As will be seen from the engraving, the church tower and spire, the design of which was once erroneously attributed to Nicholas Hawksmore, a pupil of Sir Christopher Wren, can be seen from miles away. The height of this structure is 150 feet above ground level, and it was surmounted by a weather vane in the shape of a lion.

A sandstone wall topped by ornate iron railings and punctuated by three ornamental gates, surrounded the churchyard. These were removed when the whole area was opened up in the 1970's, leaving the fine proportions of the building open to view from every angle. Aesthetically this was an imaginative piece of planning, but in the present situation the church, like many other structures, is prone to vandalism.

The War Memorial, which from the time of its erection in 1916 stood at the junction of West Street and Church Street, was moved to its present site at the time of this development, and now stands on terracing on the south side of the church.

The old Legs of Man Hotel and the Custom House were replaced by the Deanes House Hotel. Other views of the surrounding country appear at the end of this book.

Wm. Winstanleys's Prospect of Prescot.

Above: Prescot Church Circa 1920.

Prescot Church from churchyard path.
Circa 1920.

Above: View of old Church Street, showing the Legs of Man Hotel, the forerunner of the present Deanes House.

Below: Church Street from High Street corner. Circa 1920.

Left: Repair to the church spire around 1950. The weather vane had become dislodged and was awaiting reinstallation. When the lion stood alongside the base of the tower it measured three feet high by four feet long.

Below: Church Street, looking westward with the Deanes House (centre) and the old Post Office, which originally housed the Grammar School, in the foreground. Circa 1900.

Prescot War Memorial unveiled Sept. 1916. Dr Sam Green's surgery and house (Church Street) in the background.

Right: Unveiling of the War Memorial on September 9th 1916. It was originally located at the corner of Church Street and West Street.

Below: The Roman Catholic presbytery. The ambulatory (left) connects this to the church of Our Lady and Saint Joseph. Circa 1900.

Above: Corner of old Church Street opposite North Door of Church, circa 1920. Edwards boot repair shop, and Eaton's confectionery are beyond. This area is now the bus station.

Below: The Old Post Office, formerly the site of the old Grammar School, Circa 1900.

Right: East side of Church Street, viewed from the corner of West Street. Westminster Bank is in the top left-hand corner, whilst the house at the bottom was the home and surgery of Dr S.M. Green. Circa 1920.

Left: View from Market Place of southern entrance to the churchyard, circa 1920. Left of photo - Market Hall. Right of photo - Apse of Town Hall. The terracing which accommodates the War Memorial is in the centre.

# CHAPTER TWO

## Market Place, Sewell Street (Snig Lane) and Hall Lane.

Before Prescot was classified as a market town, buying and selling of cattle and agricultural produce was carried on in the vicinity of the church porch.

In due time a charter was granted in 1333, during the reign of Edward III, to William de Dacre, Rector of Prescot. It enabled him to hold a market and move-able fair in the town, to continue for three days, commencing on the Wednesday next after the Feast of Corpus Christi. Where this event was located is not clear, but as the Market Place was in close proximity to the church, it seems feasible that the fair was held here. With the passage of time this became the established site for subsequent markets and fairs. The latest of these, still remembered by some of us, was the 'Pot' or 'Mug' Fair. This was held from Shrove Tuesday onwards in Market Place until June or July.

The Georgian Town Hall was erected in 1775, and the Market Hall of later date occupied the west side of Market Place. The latter replaced the old Round House at the lower end of the street, which is depicted in the line drawing on page 24.

The Sunday School, together with other functions, was held in the Town Hall.

Prescot was unique in that it enjoyed the benefits and the privileges of a Court Leet. This, in Tudor times and beyond, made the town self-governing. It was possessed of certain exemptions from iniquitous taxes which other townships in the vicinity had to endure.

This court, in the 18th century, was a forerunner of the local government of later years. At the time of my boyhood the Court Leet had been shorn of its powers, but was preserved as a relic of past days. Nominal appointments were made, and renewed annually at a meeting in the Town Hall, which was followed by a banquet. An ancient custom which was preserved was the 'perrying of money'. Coins which had been heated were cast into Market Place from a window in the courtroom to be retrieved by the populace below. This token ceremony was continued until well into the 20th century.

Sadly, the Town Hall being in a dilapidated state, was demolished some decades ago. Efforts had been made to raise funds for its preservation, but unfortunately these failed. To the town's considerable loss, the building which was a centrepiece for the ancient township, was demolished. The Market Hall suffered a similar fate. One of the more sombre uses of the Market Hall had been to house plastic coffins in great quantity, in readiness for air-raid casualties during the blitz in World War II.

The road leading southwards from the bottom of Market Place was known as Snig Lane, and stretched as far as Prescot Hall. (see page 30). The vicar of Prescot, the Rev. Dr. Samuel Sewell (1776-1815) was a great benefactor to the town and opened the Sunday School here.

The first such Sunday School had been started in Gloucester by Robert Raikes just one year before. It celebrated its bi-centenary a few years ago. After his death, Snig Lane was renamed Sewell Street in memory of this great philanthropist.

A continuation of Sewell Street at its southern end was Hall Lane. This was obviously so-named because it led to Prescot Hall, the traditional home of the Rector of Prescot. Later this was a farm and in my day was in the tenancy of Ottiwell Ward. It later became absorbed in the complex of B.I.C.C. Ltd.

Hall Lane, just beyond the railway bridge, divides into Shaw Lane to the left, and Cross or Stank Lane to the right. This latter continues to the township of neighbouring Whiston.

Market Place, Prescot. Circa 1910.

Above: Old print of Market Place showing Round House and Stocks.

Right: The Round House (Lock-Up) at lower end of Market Place.

The 'Perrying of Money', circa 1930, a relic of the Court-Leet Ceremony.

Left: The southern aspect of the Town Hall, adjoining the south gate of the churchyard. Circa 1920.

Above: The Georgian Town Hall (now demolished) was reputed to be the finest example of this type of architecture in south-west Lancashire. Circa 1900.

Sewell Street West Side and Upper End. Circa 1926

Sewell Street No's 22/28 West side. Circa 1926

The side elevation of the Town Hall on Market Place. Note the bell tower and cupola. Circa 1930.

# CHAPTER THREE

## Kemble Street (Late Hillock Street)

On an earlier map Kemble Street is shown as Copt Holt Lane, but more recently, because it passed through Hillock Meadow, it was known as Hillock Street.

When the world-famous tragedian, John Philip Kemble, made his name on the London stage, the fact that he was born in a house in Hillock Street in 1757 was commemorated by the re-naming of what is now known as Kemble Street. Kemble became actor/manager in both Drury Lane and Covent Garden in London. The street formed part of the Turnpike Road leading through Prescot. With the development of the town this became a populous area, and in the 19th and 20th centuries it was built up along its entire length. It accommodated shops and dwelling houses, some of which are still standing at the present time.

In recent years it has, like some other parts of the town, ceased to be the prosperous centre which it once was, particularly at its eastern end, where part of B.I.C.C.'s factory has been closed.

A number of courts were located on its southern side, and, in living memory, these were centres of accommodation.

Aspinall Street, Cyprus Street, Houghton Street and Bond Street reached out from Kemble Street, whilst on the south side Station Road, Williams Street and Chester Street adjoined it.

The now disused entrance gate to B.I.C.C.'s factory replaced Young's tobacconist's shop and three houses at the corner of Pottery Place on the south side of the street. This latter, which was also known as Mughouse Wient, accommodated a number of dwellings.

To the west of this gate is the chapel of the Zion Independent Methodists. An earlier chapel of some antiquity, which in later years housed for a time the Prescot branch of the County Library, was demolished when B.I.C.C. took over the land.

Several areas of wasteland on both sides of Kemble Street reveal what is today an area of considerable decay.

Wood Street, off East Side of Sewell Street, (near the top). Circa 1926.

Rear view of Prescot Old Hall. Circa 1926.

The birthplace of John Philip Kemble 1757 - 1823 in Hillock (later Kemble) Street.

Below: The house where John Kemble was born. This has now been demolished and is part of Beaconsfield.

Above: Portrait of actor/manager John Philip Kemble.

Right: Young's tobacconist shop and several houses in Kemble Street, opposite Houghton Street, and at the corner of Pottery Place, (Mughouse Wient).

Actor J.P. Kemble as Cato, obtained from the Walker Art Gallery by Mrs P.S. Jones who reports: "This is said to be a fine likeness of Kemble, here playing the part of Cato who as such has opposed Caesar. He sits, scroll on lap and dagger on the table at his side, whilst contemplating suicide in his remorse."

Right: Property on the north side of Kemble Street, now demolished. The site has now been redeveloped to form the rear of the Prescot Centre.

Above: A decorated 'float' used in one of the many processions which followed this route in a perambulation around Prescot.

# CHAPTER FOUR

## Eccleston Street

For as long as I recall, Eccleston Street has been the main shopping centre of the town of Prescot. Formerly known as Newgate Street (and Fountain Street in an earlier age) it reaches from Church Street and Market Place in the west, to Chapel Street and Ackers Street. The road stretches beyond this point in an easterly direction. This section used to be known as Little New Road but is now styled Eccleston Street as far as its junction with Warrington Road.

There is no doubt that certain buildings of antiquity still exist in this street, although most of these have had their fronts modernised. Some months ago when a hairdressing salon on the north side was replanned, timbers of the 16th and 17th century were uncovered and refaced, but not removed. The building line on both sides remains virtually unaltered although the erection of the Prescot Centre has incurred a breach in that line for a considerable portion of the south side. The days are past when the frontage on both sides was dominated by old establishments like Hemingway's Pharmacy, The Public Benefit Boot and Shoe shop, Charlie Rimmer's Fruit and Fish shop - with Quick's the Booksellers adjoining it. These were features in the days of my youth.

Before the erection in 1922 of the Lyme House Cinema, Garratt's Drapery store and the Farmer's Stores with Hockenhull's occupied much of the area now accommodating the Prescot Centre.

On the other side, such shops as Whittle's Pork Butchery, Saunder's Green grocery, Johnson's Outfitters, Martindale's Meat Purveyors and Pegrams Stores comprised the middle part of that frontage, ending with Baker's Pawnshop at the Leyland Street intersection. Beyond this were the Argenta Meat Company, Byron's Greengrocery, Garner's Drapery and Seddon's Grocery Store.

All of these have new occupants and in some cases the businesses conducted are of a different nature.

Johnson's the Dyers were located at the corner of Atherton Street, and Frank D.A. Atherton, the chemist, had his establishment between this shop and the Wesleyan Schoolroom.

Changes in ownership and the nature of business transacted, have altered the appearance of this busy street, whilst pedestrianisation has given more ready access to the shoppers who frequent this part of the town.

Over a period of years some of the traders have disappeared completely. Williams confectionery, Peer's Butchery, Rigby's Boot Repairs, Maypole Dairy, Morris's, Quick's and many others, are now only names from the past.

It is important, I feel, to compare the situation as it is now, with the usages of yesteryear, particularly as the Prescot Centre has changed the appearance of the place still further.

Tudor Building in Eccleston Street (now Gas Showrooms) in the time of Mr Miller (Hopping Bob) who carried on business as a barber, tobacconist and booking agent for a shipping company. Circa 1915.

Above: Lyme House cinema. A popular place of entertainment for many decades. Located on south side of Eccleston Street. Circa 1922.

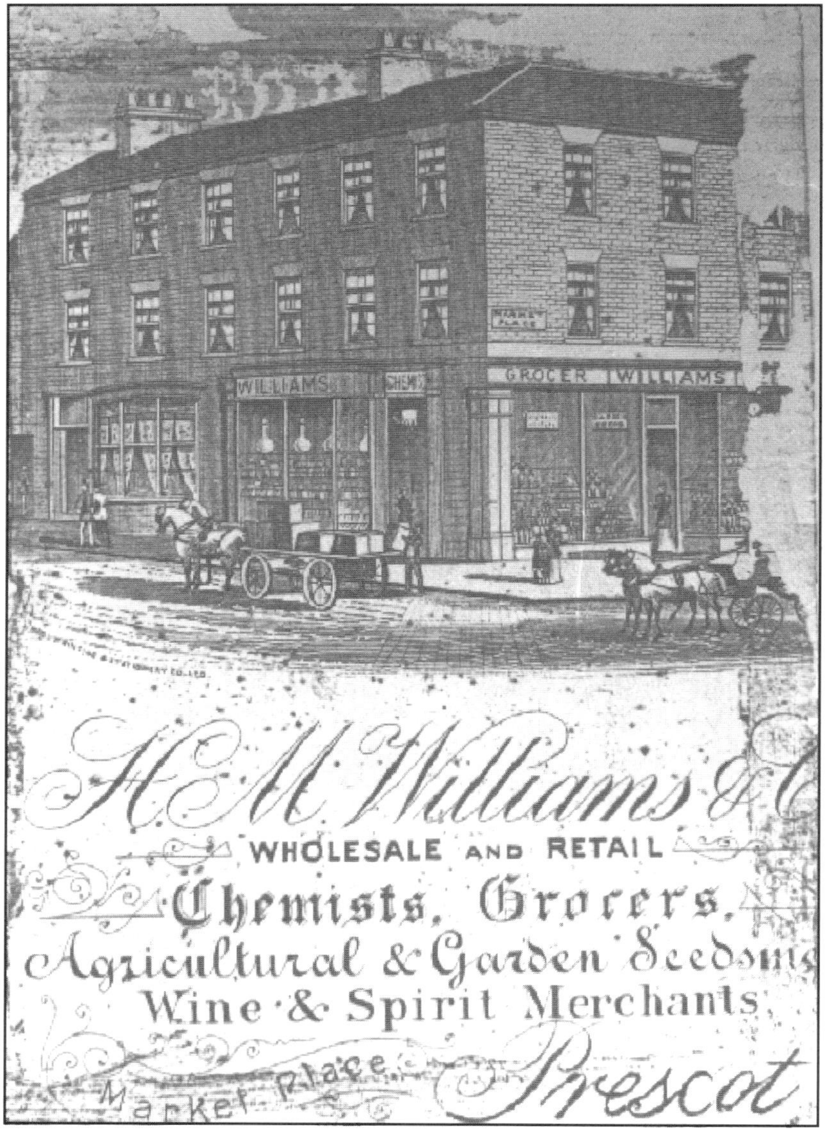


H.M. Williams, Market Place Corner, 1900.

Above: Shop of Geo. G. Hemingway, at 34 Eccleston Street, from his 1903 yearbook.

Right: Shop at corner of Eccleston Street and Atherton Street from handbook. Circa 1920.

# CHAPTER FIVE

## Derby Street

Derby Street, from Swan Hotel (off picture on left) to Police Station (just seen on right). Circa 1920.

The approach to Prescot from Liverpool Road in the west was via Derby Street. This, in its altered form, is now part of the A57. In the days when electric tramcars connected Liverpool with St. Helens, a single track with 'loops' at Knowsley Park Lane and Stanley Crescent ran along this street. The terrace, which on the north side connected Park Lane with Stanley Crescent, ended with the police station complex. On the opposite side of the street there was also a terrace at its lower end, but a number of larger houses, set back from the road, were fronted by gardens with high iron railings.

West End Villa stood at the junction of Derby Street and West Street. These were known respectively as Fall Lane and Hooley's Walk, and formed part of the turnpike Fall Lane leading to St. Helens and Ashton, and Hooley's Walk to Warrington.

Public House (Swan Hotel) at the beginning of the north side of Derby Street and at the corner of Knowsley Park Lane. Circa 1910.

Derby Street looking westward from the offices of Henry Cross and Son, Solicitors. Circa 1930

Above: South side of Derby Street, and a typical scene with a wagon pulled by four horses. View from below Stanley Crescent. Circa 1912.

Left: View from the Royal Hotel (Cab Yard) with Parr's Bank in the background. This is now the Prescot Museum. Circa 1920.

Left: The Royal Hotel in the course of demolition around 1936. Office of H.Y. Cross & Son, and gate to Parkside in the foreground left.

Above: Cottages in Parkside off Derby Street. Since demolished and now part of the extension to the solicitors office. Circa 1910.

The old Assembly Rooms. Now the site of Prescot Library, which for a time was housed in the building on the right. Circa 1936.

Houses at the rear of the Royal Hotel Yard, with the Assembly Rooms on the right and Cross's office on the left. Circa 1940.

Rear view of houses in cab yard. Circa 1930.

# CHAPTER SIX

## High Street (Fazackerley Street in earlier days)

The continuation of Derby Street was formerly known as Fazackerley Street, now the High Street, and stretched as far as the King's Arms. At this point the road divides with the road to the left leading to Eccleston Lane Ends and St. Helens, whilst the A57 continues beyond this point to Rainhill and Warrington.

A preservation order covers part of the High Street, where certain dilapidated properties await attention. Some have been tastefully refurbished. The Council Offices of the then Urban District Council stand on the site of old Fazackerley House.

Almost opposite this building was a row of houses and shops. These have now been demolished and the ground is used as a car park. The late John Garth's cornmillers establishment, in the picture below, stood midway along the High Street. It is currently a motor spares shop.

High Street, Prescot. Cottages with J. Garth's Corn Mill. Circa 1950.

Mr Garth, proprietor of the Corn Mills with Mr Metcalfe.

Prescot Urban District Council Offices. Circa 1946.

Present day Ray's Confectionery with the entrance to North Court High Street (right) circa 1930.

Prescot Grammar School. Circa 1900. Remained school until 1924. Later a clinic, until demolished. At present a car park.

Above: High Street, Prescot looking east, circa 1910.

Left: High Street, Prescot, looking westwards. Nag's Head Hotel and Atherton Street on left. Circa 1910.

Atherton Street at its junction with High Street: The King's Arms Hotel top left. Circa 1910.

Above: High Street, corner of Chapel Street: view from The King's Arms. Circa 1910.

Right: The terrace in High Street, opposite the old Conservative Club. It stood between Mill Street (right) and Stone Street, and housed the Fruit and Fishshop of C. Fowler and two old stone houses on the extreme left. Demolition took place recently and this area is now a bus stop, with a car park beyond. Another example of the changing face of the old High Street. Circa 1950.

# CHAPTER SEVEN

## Highfield Place

As the name would seem to imply, this part of Prescot enjoyed the highest elevation in the entire town.

Bordered by the rear of Church Street to the west, and Leyland Street to the east, access was possible from both High Street and Eccleston Street.

Just after the turn of the century this was a very populous area. In an earlier age it accommodated people engaged in a number of callings and professions.

From an earlier print it is clear that at least one of several windmills was located hereabouts, as the name Mill Street clearly indicates. Several attorneys had offices in Highfield Place, and Zachariah Leafe, the renowned medical man, practised here. A blacksmith's shop and a brewery were located near here. Dr. Leafe is said to have been part owner of a slave ship which was named 'The Prescot', but whether we should speak of this with pride is a matter of opinion.

Of more recent date the whole area was made up of many small cobbled streets in which houses stood cheek by jowl.

The gradual dilapidation which I remember well, was arrested when the Urban District Council built the property in the Shaw Lane area. The occupants of these houses, many of which had long been condemned, were re-accommodated in this new estate, south of the Liverpool to Wigan line of the then London and North Western Railway.

There was a larger house in this area which, as children, we referred to as Hardy's House. Whether this was used by Nelson's Flag-lieutenant, ('Kiss me, Hardy') was for many years a matter of some debate. A high sandstone wall, part of which is still standing, must have surrounded this large house.

Hill Street, facing east from Mill Street towards Stone Street. Circa 1950.

Above: Prescot watchmaker's workshop. Circa 1950.

Right: Stone Street.

Above: Highfield Place. Circa 1930.

Above: Cover Yard Circa 1930.

Right: Mill Street from Eccleston Street. Circa 1930.

Looking towards Victoria Hotel (Long Pull). Circa 1930.

# CHAPTER EIGHT

## Courts, wients, passages, yards, squares and places

In an age when Prescot was a compact town, land availability within its centre was obviously at a premium. Cottages were erected on every piece of land which became vacant. Consequently, a preponderance of these small alleys, or wients, were used for the building of small unpretentious dwellings, which in many cases, housed quite large families. This development may have been dictated by economic conditions, or a sense of fellowship within families - or both. In any event, in pre-Victorian times these cottages sprang up in what must have appeared to be the most unlikely places. Most of these dwellings have now gone, although the sites on which they were erected are in evidence even today.

At right angles to, and off Derby Street, were Golden or Gold Hand Court and West-End Cottages. The former housed people who made gold hands for watches, and was located off the south side of Derby Street, opposite what was then known as the Bank Buildings. West-End Cottages comprised of half a dozen dwellings.

Lyon's Court held three or four small houses between the Plough Hotel in Warrington Road, and the Eagle and Child Hotel at the corner of Scotchbarn Lane. Well yard was a similar collection of two or three cottages off St. Helens Road opposite the waterworks pumping station.

Barrows and Parker's Courts were located off Kemble Street, as was Pottery Place, otherwise known as Mughouse Wient. Several courts were to be found behind Houghton Street, Moss Street and Derby Street. Yates Court was off Sewell Street, and No 1 Court and Tyrer's Passage off High Street. Gaskell's Passage and Cover Yard were off Highfield Place, and Carver's Yard was between Sewell Street and Trap Lane (Garden Walk). Squire's Place and Victoria Place were off Ackers Street (The Acres). Saggerson's and Beesley Courts were off St. Helens Road and Pemberton's Court lay behind Derby Square, both of which were off Warrington Road.

Left: Barrow's Court. Off Kemble Street to the south side of the Palace Cinema. Known before 1871 as 'Bear's Paw Yard'.

Above: No 1 Court. Off High Street. Circa 1930.

West End cottages off Derby Street. Circa 1950.

Above: Lyon's Court off Warrington Road, behind the Plough Hotel and approached from the end of Scotch Barn Lane circa 1930. Known prior to 1871 as Lyon's Smithy.

Above: Golden (Gold Hand) Court, also off the south side of Derby Street and opposite the old Bank Buildings. Circa 1930.

Above: Pottery Place. Off south side of Kemble Street circa 1930. Also known prior to 1871 as the 'Tan Yard'.

Left: Well Yard, circa 1930. This yard was adjacent to several old cottages fronting that part of St. Helens Road opposite the pumping station of the old water works. Behind this yard were the farm buildings and fields of Metcalfe's Farm, now Grammar School land.

Left: North Court, in High Street between Ray's Bakery and the car park which was formerly the site of the Grammar School. Circa 1920.

Below: Carver's Yard off Market Place. Between Sewell Street and Garden Walk (Trap Lane). Circa 1920.

Right: Tyrer's Passage (Poor House Wient), circa 1920. At the side of Garth's Corn Mill, now Brook Bridge Repairs and Spares.

Below: Yates' Court, circa 1930, off west side of Sewell Street at its lower end. Known also as the 'Fold'.

Right: Gaskells passage Mill Street at Eccleston Street End Circa. 1930

Above: Cover Yard, Highfield Place. Circa 1930.

Above: Court off Derby Street.

Beesley Court by The King's Arms. Circa 1930.

# CHAPTER NINE

## St. Helens Road

From the King's Arms in Prescot, the road (which is part of the Turnpike already mentioned) leads in a north-easterly direction to St. Helens. This is an important thoroughfare, along which the old St. Helens Corporation electric trams used to ply. Originally these trams joined those of Liverpool Corporation at Knotty Ash, and later at the Prescot end of Huyton Lane. Eventually the terminus for both systems was located at the King's Arms. Electric trolley-buses superseded the trams on a circular route from St. Helens to Prescot, and on through Rainhill to join up at Toll Bar with the route to St. Helens.

Changes have taken place in St. Helens Road, Prescot, over the years, but it is mainly with the side roads that I shall deal in this account, because so many features which once dominated this area have disappeared or changed, almost beyond recognition. With the demolition of the King's Arms Hotel, a smithy of some antiquity at the end of Grosvenor Road was absorbed in the car park of the new Fusilier public house. Similarly, the premises of the old Prescot Gas Company have taken on a new appearance, as a depot for the North West Gas Board.

Left: Stone Street, with High Street in background. Circa 1930.

Above: Houses in Ward Street, off St Helens Road

Above: Back Moss Street circa 1930. This has now been absorbed in the small estate known as Seddon Court.

Above: Prescot house decorated for the Festival of Britain in 1951.

A house in Rowson Street, Prescot, decorated in fine style for the Festival of Britain, 1951.

# CHAPTER TEN

## Warrington Road

The visitor approaching Prescot from the direction of Rainhill should be excused from having a depressing opinion of the town's dereliction and neglect.

Wide spaces now mark the absence of terraces, which although not particularly attractive, at least preserved continuity in the building line. The abandonment of workshops once occupied by B.I.C.C. in its heyday, is the beginning of this decay. From the corner of Kemble Street to the bend in the road opposite Oliver Lyme Road, uncared for plots of land mark the departure of Kelly Street and East Street, whilst the destruction of terraces opposite the old 'Board' School, in which many of us received our early education, presents a dismal prospect.

It is hoped that plans for the development of this approach to Prescot are envisaged, to make attractive this important entrance to the old town.

A 1930's print showing the King's Arms Hotel and surrounding properties at the beginning of Warrington Road.

Above: The Prescot Mill, prior to 1908.

Below: Remains of the Prescot Mill after the fire of 1908.

# CHAPTER ELEVEN

## Victoria House and Beaconsfield, Houghton and Cyprus Streets

Very little remains in its original form of that part of Prescot which in my youth was an integral part of the town.

From Pottery Fields, at the corner of which the Old Mill stood (destroyed by fire in 1908) to the west side of Cyprus Street, there is little to remind us of this area as we once knew it. Only the name remains of old Ackers Street which connected Eccleston Street with Houghton Street. The roads leading off this have all but disappeared. This is certainly the case with Beaconsfield Street, Victoria Place and Albert Street, whilst one side of each of Cyprus and Houghton Streets have been absorbed in the new complex. This stretches from Pennington Gardens to Kemble Street and provides housing for countless families. However, the character of this part of the town has completely altered. Scenes from this part of Prescot are reproduced here, and they serve as reminders of what was an important part of the town earlier this century.

Gone are the old Church School, the Victoria Place Methodist Chapel, Squires Place and Albert Street, which joined Cyprus Street with Houghton Street, and housed the old Salvation Army citadel.

Old Squires Place was approached by a gate in Ackers Street. It accommodated the building yard of the firm of S. & A. Taylor. This was, in earlier times, the site of the Cuckstool Pit, where 'Scolds' were subjected to the rigours of the Ducking Stool. A sandstone wall encircled this yard, and this continued into Victoria Place, and beyond into Cyprus Street. At the present time it is used, together with part of Ackers Street, as a car park.

Warrington Road, Prescot. View looking eastwards from the King's Arms. Circa 1920.

Above: Houghton Street. Lower end entrance to yet another court. This is No 6. Circa 1926.

Right: The entrance to number 4 Court on Houghton Street's east side. Circa 1926.

Above: Back of Houghton Street, doubtless within the courts. Circa 1926

Above: Bond Street, north end abutting on Pottery Fields. Circa 1926.

Parents of Mr E. Gore. Circa 1900.

Above: Prescot Old Scouts Re-Union, 1940.

Right: Part of Mr Gore's workshop in Beaconsfield Street. Circa 1900.

Left: Mr E. Gore, Broochmaker, 1940.

Below: The Brewery, circa 1900.

Above: Ackers Street, north side. Circa 1930

Above: Squires Place, south side of Ackers Street at Chapel Street end, circa 1930. Before 1871 it was known as 'Cook Stay Nook'.

Above: Ackers Street, corner of Victoria Place. Circa 1930.

Above: Ackers Street, Eccleston Street end, south side. Circa 1930.

Above: The east side of old Houghton Street. Circa 1930. Opposite was the Church School.

# CHAPTER TWELVE

## Aspinall Street

Aspinall Street has always been a broad road leading from Atherton Street and Eccleston Street, southwards beyond Kemble Street to Station Road and thence to the railway station.

It housed, at its northernmost end, the veterinary surgeon's premises where Mr Leyland (Farrier) lived and conducted his practice. The old Congregational, now the United Reformed Church, is on the lower side of this property, and beyond that was the home and surgery of Dr G.E. (Bert) Green. The latter, who was the brother of Dr. Sam Green, the town's M.O.H. (Medical Officer of Health) was a surgeon. This building, and another similar house, brought the building line to an end. Beyond this, as far as the Crown Hotel, stretched open land known as the Old Park. This was the site of periodic travelling fun fairs, when tractors and caravans surrounded an arena of carousels and sideshows. The surface of this large piece of ground was undulating and of hard, packed clay. In wet weather it was interlaced with channels which drained off surplus water to the south. As a boy, it was always a source of wonderment to me how the operators of the fair managed to erect booths and secure the heavy traction engines. The Old Park site is today filled by a Telephone Exchange, the General Post Office and the Labour Exchange.

Opposite was the old Wire Works Club and Drill Hall, south of which the Civic Hall was erected. These have now been demolished and the land has been used for the Prescot Centre.

The block of buildings indicated on this page was variously used in the past as Frank Dickie's radio and television showroom, the N.C.B. local office and a doctor's surgery. It is now entirely occupied by a number of doctors as a medical centre.

Right: Dr Youatt occupied the lower part of this building in Aspinall Street. Later two brothers, surnamed O'Ryan, practised here. The whole building is now a medical centre in which several doctors practice.

Right: Exterior view of The Civic Hall in 1980 before its demolition.

Left: Interior of The Civic Hall which was demolished to make way for the Prescot Centre.

# CHAPTER THIRTEEN

## Reminders of a bygone age

The approaches to the town of Prescot have undergone considerable alteration in a lifetime. This is true of all sides of the town. The collection of pictures which appears in this chapter shows the degree of change which has taken place in the space of eight decades.

Huyton Lane in the days when I first knew it was, for the most part, a quiet avenue, along which traffic was limited to horsedrawn vehicles and bicycles. A motor car was a rare sight. Today, with the opening of the M57 motorway at the Prescot end, and an extensive development of property beyond Whiston Lane, it is a busy thoroughfare. The land encircling the 'Red Hazels', which recently was a teachers' training college, has been developed by the building of classrooms, living accommodation and offices. It bears little resemblance to the estate previously occupied by the Misses Pilkington. The 'Old Carrs', an area of common land has disappeared, as has the Waiting Room at the tram terminus shown on page 87.

Quarry House, at the corner of Delph Lane still stands, but the country walk known as Scotchbarn Lane has been transformed by the inclusion of dwelling houses, public baths and the large Edmund Arrowsmith school. The bowling green, and the 17th century inn of the same name, have been absorbed in a network of roads to the north of Wood Lane.

The original general office of B.I.C.C. has been superseded by a newer office block located on Bridge Road. Two decades ago the B.I.C.C. factory, which employed many thousands of people from Prescot and the surrounding area, dominated the town. It is now but a shadow of its former self. Buildings have been demolished or are in the process of being discarded. On the north side, a ring road has marginally reduced the spread of Knowsley Park, and the once thriving nursery of James Whitaker & Son has all but disappeared.

It is to be hoped that plans are in hand, following the fine start made by the developers of the Prescot Centre, which will reverse this dereliction.

Left: The Carrs pre-1908.

Right: The Carrs Cottage

Above: The Church on the hill,
Prescot. Circa 1908-1912.

Below: Huyton Lane, Prescot. Circa 1920.

Above: Huyton Lane, Prescot looking east. Circa 1920.

Above: Waiting Room, Huyton Lane. Circa 1920

Left: Prescot from the wood. Circa 1920.

Below: Bowling Green Team, 1908.

Left: Bowling Green Inn, 1908.

Left: Quarry House at the corner of Delph Lane and Two Butt Lane. Circa 1920.

Above: Scotchbarn Lane. Circa 1920.

Right: Tinling's outing to Blackpool lights, circa 1930, waiting on Prescot Station.

Below: Aerial View of Prescot, between 1930 - 1950.

Right: The British Insulated Callender Cables (BICC), Ltd, 1926.

# INDUSTRIES

## Coal-Mining

After agriculture, one of the earliest sources of employment in the town of Prescot was the development of coal-mining. At first the produce was absorbed by domestic use only, but as the extent of the coalfield was realised this developed into a much wider trade, occasioning the construction of the turnpike road to Liverpool.

## Pottery

The clay dug hereabouts was particularly suitable for the manufacture of coarse earthenware such as conical sugar-moulds and pan-mugs. The latter were of such high quality as to give rise to the well-known slogan 'Prescot for Pan Mugs'.

## Other early trades

A gazetteer of Lancashire, compiled in 1825, speaks of the industrious nature of the people of this fast-growing township. Clock-makers, clog and pattern-makers, corn-millers, boot and shoemakers, earthenware manufacturers, woollen drapers and hosiers, mercers, nail-makers, sail-makers and saddlers were included. In addition, file cutters were here in abundance.

## Watch-making

In the gazetteer of 1825 the following trades were listed. Watch balance-makers - 7, watch pillary-makers - 2, watch hand-makers - 7, watch material-makers - 5, watch verge-makers - 5, watch movement-makers - 15 and watch tool-makers - 12. This marks the incidence of an industry for which Prescot became known world wide. In 1889, when economic conditions brought about a decline in this cottage industry, the British Watch Company (later known as The Lancashire Watch Company) came into being. The factory, which covered $11^1/_2$ acres, was erected, and 700 people were employed here. This factory used engines invented by John Wyke, a Prescot clock-maker and Joshua Hewitt, an inventor whose family were closely connected with this new enterprise. The factory, which still stands, ceased to function for the purpose of watch-making in the early part of the present century.

## File-cutting

In 1795 a note quoted Prescot files as being the 'best in the world'. It was in 1864 that 22-year-old James Blundell founded the firm which still operates today, and incorporated the use of file-cutting machines. Hitherto, files had been cut by hand, the makers operating in small galleries attached to their dwelling houses. Long hours worked for a relatively poor return caused these workers to be known as 'poverty knockers'.

## Horticulture

Several nurseries existed in the town, the most successful of which was the firm James Whitaker & Sons, whose tomato and house plants were in great demand.

## Cable-making

Throughout my lifetime the name Prescot has been synonymous with cable-making. The world-renowned British Insulated Callender Cable Co. Ltd, began here as the Prescot Wire Company. The number employed when I worked for this company was, in Prescot alone, well in excess of 10,000, and a wide variety of electrical components, as well as many types of electric cables, were produced here.

## Postscript

Watch-making in Prescot has sadly disappeared. And the transfer of part of the works of B.I.C.C. has reduced the work force here very appreciably. As a result, the change in the appearance of the town is most marked.

Throughout its long history Prescot has been a place of great industrial importance, and as has been well said, 'The skills and inventiveness, bred out of numerous cottage industries and back garden workshops, contributed to the later progress of mankind in commercial and industrial enterprise'. But Prescot's citizen's influence has by no means been stifled. It is merely being put to the test.

Like many a noble edifice, Prescot Parish Church has suffered the ravages of time and weather. Its absent clock, a virtual landmark, has been a source of regret and annoyance for some time past. The church authorities are very conscious of the need for urgent action, but vast sums of money will be required to complete this work. Appeals are being launched by the Parochial Church Council and the Prescot Church Preservation Society, a non-sectarian organisation working in close conjunction with the former.

The matter is well in hand, but an appreciable amount of work is required to be done on the structure of the tower and spire.

Until this is completed the fittings cannot be reinstated, so the more quickly sufficient money is forthcoming, the sooner will the work be done.

May all who regard Prescot as their home town continue to find frequent opportunities to quote and apply that unfailing password to further success and achievement:

"FLOREAT PRESCOTIA"

# INDEX

Abraham, Mavis, Miss, 7
Ackers Street, 35, 37, 73, 79, 80, 81
Acres, The, 57
Aerial View of Prescot, 87
Agriculture, 91
Air Raids, 22
Albert Street, 73
Alice Roberts, Mrs, 7
Alison J. Bibby, Miss, 7
Argenta Meat Company, 35
Arrowsmith, Edmund Sch, 84
Ashton Cross, 11
Ashton-in-Makerfield, 11, 40
Aspinall Street, 3, 29, 82
Assembly Rooms, 46
Atherton, F.D. Chemist, 35
Atherton Street, 35, 29, 49, 50, 82
A57, 11, 40, 46

Baines, History of Lancashire, 9
Back Houghton Street, 75
Back Moss Street, 68
Baker, T. Pawnbroker, 35
Bank Building, 57, 60
Bank Quay, Warrington, 11
Barrow's Court, 57, 58
Beaconsfield Street, 3, 32, 73
Bear's Paw Yard, 58
Beesley Court, 65
B.I.C.C. Ltd, 23, 29, 71, 84, 92
Bird i'th Hand, 11
Blacklow Brow, 11
Blue Bell, 11
Blundell, James 91
Bold Heath, 11
Bond Street, 29, 75
Boot and Shoemakers, 91
Bowling Green, Wood Lane, 84, 87
Brewery, The, 78
Board School, 71
British Watch Company, 91
Broad Green, 11
Brook Bridge, 11
Brown, J.A, Outfitter, 39
Bus Station, 20
Bygroves, Bill, 7
Byron, William, Greengrocer, 35

Cable-making, 92
Cub Yard, 45
Carver's Yard, 57, 62
Cato, 33
Ceasar, 33
Chapel Street, 35, 50, 80
Charles Rimmer, 35
Chester Diocese, 9
Chester Street, 29
Churchley, 9
Churchley Fields, 9
Church on the Hill, 86
Church Porch, 22
Church School, 73, 80
Church Spire, 17
Church Street, 14, 16, 17, 18, 19, 20, 21, 35, 52
Churchyard, 14, 15, 21, 26
Citadel, Salvation Army, 73
Civic Hall, 82, 83
Clark, Dave, 7
Clinic, 48
Clock-making, 91
Clog-making, 91
Coal-mining, 91
Cot, Cote, or Coit, 9
Congregational Church, 82
Conservative Club, 51
Cook Stay Nook, 8
Coombs Walter, 7
Copt Holt, 11
Copt Holt Lane, 29
Corn Milling, 47, 91
Corpus Christi, Feast, 22
Courts, 3, 29, 57
Court Leet, 22, 25
Cover Yard, 55, 57, 64
Cropper's Hill , 11
Cross Lane, 23
Crown Hotel, 82
Cuckstool Pit, 73
Cupola, 28
Custom House, 14
Cyprus Street, 29, 73

Deanes House Hotel, 14, 17
Decorated Float, 34
De Dacre, William, 22
Delph Lane, 84, 89
Derby Square, 57
Derby Street, 3, 40, 41, 42, 43, 46,
57, 59, 60
Dickie, Frank, 82
Ditton, 9
Drill Hall, 82
Ducking Stool, 73
Duckworth, Ralph, 9
Dyers, Johnson, 35

Eagle and Child, Hotel, 57
Eaton's Confectionery, 20
Earthenware, 91
East Street, 71
Ecclesiastical Parish, 9
Eccleston Arms, 11

# INDEX


Eccleston Hill, 11
Eccleston Lane Ends, 11, 46
Eccleston Street, 3, 6, 35, 37, 39, 52, 55, 64, 73, 81, 82
Edwards, Boots Repairs, 20
Edwards, Harvey, 7
Edward, King IIIrd, 22
Electric Tramways, 40, 66

Fall Lane, 40
Farmer's Stores, 35
Fazackerley House, 46
Fazackerley Street, 46
File Cutting, 91
Floreat Prescotia, 9, 92
Fountain Street, 35
Fowler, C. Greengrocer, 51
Fold, The, 63

Garden Walk, 57, 62
Garner's Drapers, 35
Garratt's Drapers, 35
Garth, John, 46, 47
Gaskell's Passage, 57, 64
Gas Showrooms, 36
General Office, B.I.C.C. Ltd, 89
General Post Office, 82
Gloucester, 23
Glover, Harry, 7
Goddard, Steve, Media Services, 2, 17
Golden, (Gold Hand) Court, 57, 60
Gore, E. Broochmaker, 78
Gore's Parents, 76
Gore's Workshop, 77
Grammar School, Old, 17
Grammar School, (original), 20
Great Sankey, 9, 11
Green, Dr. 'Bert', Surgeon, 82
Green, Dr. Sam, M.O.H. 18, 21, 82
Green Dragon Hotel, 11
Grosvenor Road, 66

Hackley Moss, 11
Hall Lane, 3, 22, 23
Hardy's House, 52
Hawksmore, Nicholas, 14
Hemingway, G.G. Pharmacist, 7, 35, 39
Henry Cross & Son, Solicitors, 41, 43, 45
Hewitt, Joshua, 91
High Street, 3, 16, 46, 49, 50, 52, 57, 58, 62, 67
Highfield Place, 3, 52, 54, 64
Hill Street, 52
Hillock Street, 29, 31
Hillock Meadow, 29
Hockenhull, Jeweller, 35
Hooley's Walk, 40
Hopping Bob, 36
Horticulture, 92
Hosiers, 91
Houghton Street, 29, 32, 57, 73, 74, 80
Howarth, George, Rt. Hon, 5
Huyton, 9
Huyton Lane, 66, 84, 86, 87

Industries, 3, 91

James Whitaker & Sons, 84, 92
Johnson's Dyers, 35
Johnson's Outfitters, 35
Judgefield Brow, 11

Kelly Street, 71
Kemble, John, Philip, 29, 31, 32, 33
Kemble Street, 3, 29, 31, 34, 57, 58, 61, 71, 73, 82
Kenwright's Cross, 11
King's Arms, 11, 46, 51, 65, 66, 73
King's Arms Hotel, 50, 66, 71
Kings College, Cambridge, 9, 10
King Edward IIIrd, 22
King Henry VIth, 9, 10
Kitt's Bridge, 11
Knotty Ash, 11, 66
Knowles, Jack, (the late), 7
Knowsley, Metropolitan Borough, 9
Knowsley Park, 84
Knowsley Park Lane, 40, 41

Labour Exchange, 82
Lancashire Life Magazine, 7
Lancashire Watch Company, 91
Leafe, Dr. Zacharia, 52
Legs of Man Hotel, 14, 16
Ley or Leigh, 9
Leyland Street, 35, 52
Leyland (Warrier) Vet, 82
Library Service, Knowsley, 7
Lichfield Diocese, 9
Little New Road, 35
Liverpool, 91
Liverpool Archdeaconry, 9
Liverpool Diocese, 9
Liverpool Corporation Tramways, 40, 66
Liverpool Exchange, 11
Liverpool Road, 40
Liverpool - Wigan Line, 52
Local Studies Section, Huyton, 7
L.N.W. Railway, 52
London Stage, 29, 31
Lord of the Manor, 9
Lund, Bill, 7
Lyme House Cinema, 35, 37
Lyons Court, 57, 60
Lyons Smithy, 60

# INDEX


Market Hall, 21, 22
Market Place, 3, 21, 22, 23, 24, 28, 35, 38, 62
Martindale, Butcher, 35
Maypole Dairy, 35
Mercers, 91
Mersey, River, 9
Metcalfe, Mr, 47
Metcalf Ray, 7
Midland Bank Ltd, 36
Mill, after the fire, 73
Mill Lane, 56
Miller, Mr (Hopping Bob), 36
Mill Street, 51, 52, 55
Morris's Butchers, 35
Moss Street, 57
Mug or Pot Fair, 22
Mughouse Wient, 29, 32, 57
M57 Motorway, 84

Nag's Head Hotel, 49
Nail-Makers, 91
National Galleries & Museums, 7
Nelson's Flag Lieutenant, 52
Newgate Street, 35
No.1 Court, 57, 58
North Court, 48, 61
No.4 Court, 74

Old Carr's, 84, 85
Old Park, 82
Old Post Office, 17
Old Scout Re-union, 77
Old Swan, 11
Oliver Lyme, 71
Ormskirk, 9
O'Ryan, Drs, 82
Ottiwell Ward, 23
Our Lady & St. Joseph's Church, 19

Page Moss, 11
Palace Cinema, 68
Pan-mugs, 91
Parker's Court, 57
Parish Church, 14
Parochial Church Council, 92
Parr's Bank, 42
Parr Hall, 11
Parkside, 43
Pattern-making, 91
Peer's Butchery, 35
Pegram's Stores, 35
Pemberton's Court, 57
Pennington''s Gardens, 73
Pennington, W, 7
Perrying of Money, 22, 25
Petticoat Lane, 11
Plastic Coffins, 22
Plough Hotel, 57, 60
Police Station, 40
Poor House Wient, 63
Pottery, 91
Pottery Fields, 73, 74
Potterty Place, 29, 32, 59, 61
Poverty Knockers, 91
Prestbytery, 19
Prescot, 8, 9, 10, 12, 22, 34, 57, 73, 84, 91, 92
Prescot Centre, 1, 7, 34, 35, 82, 83
Prescot Church, 15, 92
Prescot Church Preservation Society, 92
Prescot for Pan-mugs, 91
Prescot Deanery, 9
Prescot Files, 91
Prescot Gas Company, 66
Prescot Hall, 9, 22, 23, 30
Prescot Hall Farm, 22
Prescot Grammar School, 9, 48, 61
Prescot Historic Society, 7
Prescot Library, 44
Prescot Manor (Ancient), 9
Prescot Mill, 72
Prescot Museum, 42
Prescot Rectory, 9
Prescot Reporter, 7
Prescot Station, 89
Prescot Urban District Council, 46, 52
Prescot, When I was a Boy, 2
Prescotacota, 9
Priestcote, 9
Public Benefit Boot & Shoe Company, 35

Quarry House, 84, 89
Quick, W.H. Bookseller, 7, 35

Rainford, 9
Rainhill, 46, 66, 71
Rainhill Stoops, 11
Ray's Confectionery, 48, 62
Rector of Prescot, 9, 22, 23
Red Hazels, 84
Rev. Robert Raikes, 23
Rev. Robert Sturman, 9
Rev. Dr. Samuel Sewell, 22
Rigby, Boot Repairs, 35
Ring Road, 66
Roby, 11
Round House, 22, 24
Rowson Street, 70
Royal Hotel, 42, 43, 45

# INDEX

Saddlers, 91
Saggerson's Court, 59
Sankey, 9
Sail-Making, 91
Saunder's Greengrocery, 35
S & A Taylor, Builders, 73
Scolds, 73
Scotchbarn Lane, 57, 60, 84, 89
Scragg, T.W, 7
Seddons, Grocers, 35
Sewell Street, 3, 22, 23, 27, 30, 57, 62
Shearwater, 1, 7
St. Helens, 11, 40, 46, 66
St. Helens Corporation, 66
St. Helens Road, 3, 57, 61, 66, 67
Stank Lane, 23
Stanley Crescent, 40, 42
Station Road, 29, 82
Stocks, 23
Stone Sreet, 51, 52, 53, 67
Strettle's Smithy, 66
Shaw, David, 7
Shaw Lane, 52
Shrove Tuesday, 22,
Snig Lane, 22, 34
South-West Lancashire, 26
Sunday School, 22, 23
Squire's Place, 57, 73, 80
Sugar Moulds, 91
Swan Hotel, 40, 41

Tan Yard, 67
Taylor, Bert, 7
Telephone Exchange, 82
Tinling's Outing, 89
Toll Bar, 66
Town Hall Apse, 21
Town Hall Georgian, 22, 26, 28
Tudor Times, 22
Tudor Building, 36
Tram Terminus Waiting Room, 84, 87
Trap Lane, 57, 62
Turnpike Road, 2, 11, 29, 66, 91
Turnpike Trust, 11
Twig Lane, 11
Two Butt Lane, 89
Tyrer's Passage, 57, 63

United Reformed Church, 82
Unveiling of War Memorial, 18
Urban District Council, 46, 47

Victoria Hotel, 56
Victoria House, 73
Victoria Place, 57, 73, 80
Victoria Place Methodist Chapel, 73

Walker Art Gallery, 7, 33
Walton, 9
War Memorial, 14, 18, 19, 21
Ward Street, 67
Warrington, 9, 11, 40, 46
Warrington Road, 3, 35, 57, 60, 71, 73
Waterworks Pumping Station, 57
Watch-Making, 53, 91, 92
Watch Balance-Makers, 91
Watch Hand-Makers, 91
Watch Material-Makers, 91
Watch Movement-Makers, 91
Watch Pillar-Makers, 91
Watch Tool-Makers, 91
Well Yard, 57, 61
West End Cottages, 57, 59
West End Villa, 40
Wesleyan Schoolroom, 35
West Street, 19
Westminster Bank Ltd, 2
Whiston, 23
Whiston Lane, 84
Whittle's Pork Butchery, 35
Wigan, 9
William's Confectionery, 35
William Street, 29
Williams, H.M. Chemist, 37
Windmill, 52
Winwick, 9
Wire-Works Club, 82
Whitaker, K.H. Dental Surgeon, 36
Wood Street, 30
Wood Lane, 84
Woollen Drapers, 91
Wren, Sir Christopher, 14
Wyke, John, 91

Yates Court, 57, 63
Youatt, Dr., 82
Young Tobacconist, 29, 32

Zion Independent Methodist Chapel, 29